Instant Pot Cookbook For Two

The Perfect Guide to 50 Quick, Easy, Healthy and Delicious Recipes

Nancy Brown

Table of Content

Introduction 5

Breakfast Recipes 6

    Recipe 1: Delicious Steamed Artichokes 7

    Recipe 2: Scotch Country Eggs 9

    Recipe 3: Butter Liver Spread 11

    Recipe 4: Spicy Apple Butter 13

    Recipe 5: Eggplant Paste 15

    Recipe 6: Chinese Style Tea Eggs 17

    Recipe 7: Marinated Artichokes 19

    Recipe 8: Bacon Egg Muffins 21

    Recipe 9: Honey Poached Pears 23

    Recipe 10: Pearl Onions 25

    Recipe 11: Mixed Vegetable Medley 27

    Recipe 12: Salsa Shredded Chicken 29

    Recipe 13: Sweet Glazed Meatloaf 31

    Recipe 14: Fresh Berry Compote 33

Lunch Recipes 35

    Recipe 15: Pork Coarse Roast 37

    Recipe 16: Green Onion Chicken 39

    Recipe 17: Italian Tenderloin Pork 41

    Recipe 18: Yummy Barbecue Beef 43

    Recipe 19: Lime Chicken Sauce 45

    Recipe 20: Barbeque Chicken Curry 47

    Recipe 21: Mixed Pepper Salad 49

    Recipe 22: Chicken Okra Soup 51

    Recipe 23: Ground Kale Soup 53

    Recipe 24: Vegetable Duck 55

    Recipe 25: Mushroom Broth Soup 57

    Recipe 26: Indian Style Goat Meat 59

    Recipe 27: Tasty Pineapple Spare Ribs 61

    Recipe 28: Butter Coconut Chicken 63

    Recipe 29: Pepper Chicken Curry 65

    Recipe 30: Boiled Sweet Potatoes 67

    Recipe31: Pumpkin Puree 69

Dinner Recipes...70

    Recipe 32: Vinegar Chicken 71

    Recipe 33: Chicken Cola Wings..73

    Recipe 34: Hot Honey Drumstick...75

    Recipe 35: Salt Roasted Chicken..77

    Recipe 36: Herb Turkey Thighs 79

    Recipe 37: Barbeque Pork 81

    Recipe 38: Bell Kabadiya Sausage..83

    Recipe 39: Chile Posole Beer 85

    Recipe 40: Vegan Chickpea Curry..87

    Recipe 41: Green Chicken Thighs 89

    Recipe 42 Coconut Meatloaf 91

    Recipe 43: Red Borscht Soup...93

    Recipe 44: Leafy Spinach Soup 95

    Recipe 45: Vegetable Spice Soup..97

    Recipe 46: Red Cabbage Salad...99

    Recipe 47: Tasty Fruit Soup 101

    Recipe 48: Anise Chicken Honey..103

    Recipe 49: Korean Chicken Thighs...105

    Recipe 50: Pork Loin with Onion Sauce 107

Conclusion 109

Introduction

Congratulations for choosing this Instant Pot Cookbook with 50 Incredible Recipes and welcome to the platform of talented chefs who are looking for a simple, easy and efficient recipes, which can be made without much difficulty. In essence, pot cooking really isn't a diet; it's a lifestyle to improve health and minimize the risk of chronic diseases that plague the whole world today. There are so many different types of benefits of the safe ways to cook recipes, but due to lack of awareness, people are missing to learn the real easy way of cooking delicious instant pot recipes.

This book has 50 tasty and friendly recipes with easy to follow step-by-step directions and nutritional information is based on a 2000 calorie diet plan. There are some ways to make delicious and nutritious recipes in a pretty short time without much effort than simply adding bunches of ingredients willy-nilly. So, to avoid this, in the following chapters, I will explain each and every step of preparation method including its health benefits and nutritional information.

Before you get started, make sure that you learn different types of helpful tricks and tips to ensure that you can cook safely and as quickly and easily as possible. These recipes ensure that you will definitely make delicious dishes in lesser time without difficulty.

Instant Pot recipe creates independence and freedom to complete the cooking tasks on your own. It allows you to learn new things and expands your palate.

The key to successfully start cooking is learning everything that you can do within your ability with a strong mind and the well instructed tasty recipes will help you be able to follow the steps closely.

Breakfast Recipes

Recipe 1: Delicious Steamed Artichokes

Ingredients

- Medium Artichokes 2
- Lemon 1
- Mayonnaise 28g
- Dijon mustard 5g
- Paprika to taste

Preparation Method

1. Add 240ml of water to the instant cooker pot and carefully lower the steamer basket inside.
2. Place artichokes facing upwards and then spritz any remaining lemon on top of each.
3. Select a cooking time for 10 minutes at high pressure. When time is up, open the pressure cooker with the natural release method.
4. Mix mayonnaise with mustard and place in a small dipping container, and then sprinkle with paprika. Serve warm and enjoy the taste.

Nutritional Information

- Preparation Time: 25 minutes
- Total Servings: 2
- Calories: 77.5
- Calories from Fat: 34
- Fat: 5g
- Saturated Fat: 4.8g
- Cholesterol: 31mg

- Total Carbohydrates: 7.1g
- Fiber: 3.5g
- Sugar: 0g
- Protein:2g

Tips to extra flavor

- Use mayonnaise as a dipping sauce for extra delicious taste

Recipe 2: Scotch Country Eggs

Ingredients

- Large eggs 2
- Country style ground sausage 250g
- Vegetable oil 10g
- Water 150ml

Preparation Method

1. Place your steamer basket in your instant pot cooker; add 240ml of water along with eggs. Select 6 minutes cooking time.
2. When the timer beeps, select a quick pressure release and carefully remove the lid. Remove the steamer basket from the pressure cooker pot. Put eggs in cold water to cool.
3. When the eggs are cool, remove the shells. Divide the sausage into four equal pieces. Flatten each piece into a flat round. Place the hard-boiled egg in the center and gently wrap the sausage around the egg.
4. Heat your instant cooking pot on sauté or browning. When the pot is hot, add oil and brown the scotch eggs on four sides.
5. Remove the scotch eggs from the pot and add 240ml water. Put a rack in the instant cooking pot and place the scotch eggs on the rack.
6. Select high pressure for 6 minutes. When the pressure is released, carefully remove and enjoy the taste.

Nutritional Information

- Preparation Time: 30 minutes
- Total Servings: 2

- Amount per Serving: 1
- Calories: 659
- Calories from Fat: 485
- Fat: 53.9g
- Saturated Fat: 13.5g
- Cholesterol: 323mg
- Carbohydrates: 16.6
- Fiber: 0.9g
- Sugar: 2.1g
- Protein:25.9g

Tips to extra flavor

- Make sure that boiled egg stays in water for at least 2 minutes before removing shells

Recipe 3: Butter Liver Spread

Ingredients

- Chicken liver 150g
- Chopped onion 1
- Bay leaf 1
- Vinegar 10g
- Anchovies 2 (which are stored in oil)
- Capers 10g
- Vegetable butter 10g
- Salt and pepper to taste

Preparation Method

1. Set your instant pot cooker to sauté mode and add olive oil, onions with a little salt and pepper, then add the chicken livers and bay leaf.
2. Select instant pot cooker timer to 5 minutes. After 5 minutes, open the lid and add red wine and mix well with a wooden spoon.
3. Again, set your instant pot cooker timer for 5 minutes at high pressure by selecting a natural release, remove and discard the bay leaf and add the anchovies and capers.
4. Blend the contents using a blender, add seasoning, vegetable butter and mix well until it mixed well.
5. Transfer to a serving container and sprinkle with your favorite fresh herbs.

Nutritional Information

- Preparation Time: 15 minutes
- Total Servings: 2
- Calories: 139

- Calories from Fat: 87
- Fat: 9.7g
- Saturated Fat: 5.6g
- Cholesterol: 158mg
- Carbohydrates: 4.2g
- Fiber: 0.6g
- Sugar: 2.1g
- Protein: 7.1g

Tips to extra flavor

- For more delicious taste, add 10 grams of purified butter

Recipe 4: Spicy Apple Butter

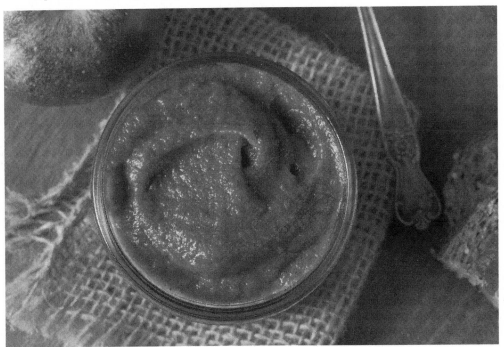

Ingredients

- Apples 2
- Water 240ml
- Cinnamon 5g
- Nutmeg 2g
- Raw honey 14g
- Pumpkin pie spice 5g

Preparation Method

1. At first, fill your instant pot with apples and add 240ml water.
2. Adjust your instant pot to steam setting and set the timer for 4 minutes.
3. When it finishes, leave it for 10 minutes or until pressure releases naturally.
4. Open the lid and using a blender, blend the apples until it reaches the consistency of butter.
5. Now, add cinnamon, raw honey to taste. Additionally, you can add nutmeg and pumpkin pie spice for extra taste.
6. Fill the apple butter in a jar and water bath for 25 minutes.
7. Now, delicious apple butter is ready; you can spread over pancakes or waffles and enjoy the taste.

Nutritional Information

- Preparation Time: 45 minutes
- Total Servings: 2
- Calories: 34
- Calories from Fat: 0g

- Fat: 0g
- Saturated Fat: 0g
- Cholesterol: 0g
- Carbohydrates: 9g
- Fiber: 0.5g
- Sugar: 8.3g
- Protein: 1g

Tips to extra flavor

- Use blender only when it becomes cold

Recipe 5: Eggplant Paste

Ingredients

- Olive oil 55g
- Eggplant 300g
- Garlic 2 cloves
- Salt 2g
- Water 105ml
- Lemon juice 10ml
- Tahini 1g
- Black olives 10g
- Fresh thyme 5g
- Fresh extra virgin olive oil (topping)

Preparation Method

1. At first, remove the skin of eggplant using peeler and slice into big chunks as possible to fill the bottom of instant pot cooker.
2. Keep the instant pot cooker on medium heat and add the olive oil. When the oil has heated, carefully add the chunks of eggplant and fry until it is caramelized on one side, approximately it will take 5 minutes, and add garlic cloves without removing the skin, salt, and water.
3. Set your instant pot cooker timer to 3 minutes at high pressure.
4. When it is finished, remove the extra water (brown liquid) from the cooker.
5. Now, add the tahini, lemon juice, cooked and garlic cloves and black olives and blend everything together using and blender.
6. Pour into the serving dish and sprinkle with fresh thyme, remaining black olives and a dash of fresh olive oil before serving.

Nutritional Information

- Preparation Time: 23 minutes
- Total Servings: 2
- Calories: 155.5
- Calories from Fat: 34
- Fat: 11.7g
- Saturated Fat: 1.8g
- Cholesterol: 0mg
- Carbohydrates: 16.8g
- Fiber: 4.5g
- Sugar: 5.6g
- Protein: 2g

Tips to extra flavor

- Before serving, sprinkle with freshly chopped parsley and cilantro

Recipe 6: Chinese Style Tea Eggs

Ingredients

- Hard-boiled eggs 2
- Soy Sauce 20g
- Lemon zest 10g
- Black tea bags 1
- Powdered cloves 5g
- Black peppercorns 10g
- Juniper berries 10g
- Bay leaves 2
- Water 280ml

Preparation Method

1. Crack the shell of the hard-boiled egg using a teaspoon (just tap them) and set aside.
2. Take one separate pan; add all of the ingredients including 240ml of water except the soy sauce.
3. Bring to a boil, and then add the soy sauce, eggs and any additional water (if necessary).
4. Cover it with tin foil. Prepare your instant pot cooker by adding 240ml of water, and placing a steamer basket inside it.
5. Set your instant pot cooker timer for 20 minutes. When the time is up, remove tin foil and let cool further.
6. Serve with shell and let your guests peel it and enjoy the taste.
7. Optional: eggs can be stored in the refrigerator in a plastic bag or darkened even further stored in the tea mixture.

Nutritional Information

- Preparation Time: 34 minutes
- Total Servings: 2
- Calories: 76
- Calories from Fat: 45
- Fat: 5g
- Saturated Fat: 1.6g
- Cholesterol: 186mg
- Carbohydrates: 1.2g
- Fiber: 0.3g
- Sugar: 0.4g
- Protein: 6.6g

Tips to extra flavor

- Don't open the shells until you serve

Recipe 7: Marinated Artichokes

Ingredients

- Large artichokes 2
- Fresh lemon juice 15g
- Balsamic vinegar 5g
- Olive oil 25ml
- Dried oregano 5g
- Garlic 2 cloves
- Sea salt 2g
- Fresh ground black pepper 2g
- Water 280ml

Preparation Method

1. At first, wash artichokes under cold water and cut off the top inch of the artichoke.
2. Place your artichokes in the inner pot of the instant pot cooker with 480ml of water. Select steam mode and reduce cooking time to 8 minutes.
3. On the other side prepare the marinade by mixing lemon juice, balsamic vinegar, olive oil, oregano, garlic, salt, and pepper in a small jar; mix well until it incorporates all ingredients and set aside.
4. Remove the artichokes from the pot and cut into half. Remove the center cone of purple prickly leaves.
5. Sprinkle the marinade over the warm artichoke and let it sit for 30 minutes to overnight.
6. When ready to serve, grill for 3 to 5 minutes and serve.

Nutritional Information

- Preparation Time: 10 minutes
- Total Servings: 2
- Calories: 204
- Calories from Fat: 124
- Fat: 13.8g
- Saturated Fat: 1.9g
- Cholesterol:0mg
- Carbohydrates: 19.3g
- Fiber: 8.9g
- Sugar: 2g
- Protein: 5.5g

Tips to extra flavor

- Don't forget to marinate overnight for delicious flavor and taste

Recipe 8: Bacon Egg Muffins

Ingredients

- Large eggs 2
- Lemon pepper 2g
- Chopped green onion half
- Cooked bacon slices 2
- Water 250ml

Preparation Method

1. At first, place a steamer basket inside instant pot cooker and add 360ml water.
2. Slowly break eggs into a large and add lemon pepper, beat well until it looks nice texture.
3. Now, divide bacon and green onion evenly between the 4 silicone muffin cups. Pour the beaten eggs into each muffin cup.
4. Place muffin cups slowly in a steamer basket and set the timer for 8 minutes. When the timer beeps, wait for natural pressure release (approximately two minutes) and lift out the steamer basket, and remove muffin cups.
5. Serve immediately with extra cream on top.

Nutritional Information

- Preparation Time: 10 minutes
- Total Servings: 2
- Calories: 147
- Calories from Fat: 52
- Fat: 3.8g
- Saturated Fat: 1.1g

- Cholesterol: 157mg
- Carbohydrates: 5g
- Fiber: 1.3g
- Sugar: 2.9g
- Protein: 15.6g

Tips to extra flavor

- Make sure that, you fill the muffin cups to about ¾ full

Recipe 9: Honey Poached Pears

Ingredients

- Lemon 1
- Water 2 cups
- White vinegar 1 cups
- Cinnamon sticks 3
- Bartlett pears 2

Honey Sauce:

- Raw honey 50g
- Coconut milk 60ml
- Coconut oil 20ml
- Maple syrup 20ml

Preparation Method

1. At first, add water, honey, cinnamon sticks and wine, to your instant pot cooker and select a warm option to make hot syrup.
2. On the other hand, peel the pears, and squeeze lemon juice. Slowly drop pears into hot syrup and cook for 3 minutes on high pressure.
3. After 3 minutes, carefully remove the pears with a slotted spoon and add syrup on pears.
4. To prepare the honey sauce for pears, put honey in saucepan d bring to boil, when it hot, add coconut milk, oil, maple syrup.
5. Before serving, cut the bottom of pears (to make it stand on the plate) and pour the warm honey sauce over. Enjoy the taste.

Nutritional Information

- Preparation Time: 10 minutes
- Total Servings: 2
- Calories: 400
- Calories from Fat: 43
- Fat: 4.8g
- Saturated Fat: 2.1g
- Carbohydrates: 65.2g
- Fiber: 6.2g
- Sugar: 45.4g
- Protein: 4g

Tips to extra flavor

- Cut bottom of pears to make it stand properly in plate

Recipe 10: Pearl Onions

Ingredients

- Cipolline 200g
- Water 100ml
- Bay leaf 1
- Salt to taste
- Balsamic Vinegar 28ml
- Honey 10g
- Coconut flour 10g

Preparation Method

1. At first, cut the both ends of the onions and clean. Place the onions in instant pot cooker and add 125ml of water, salt and bay leaf to taste.
2. Adjust cooker timer for 5 minutes on low pressure.
3. On the other hand, make the sweet and sour sauce for onions. Take small saucepan; add honey, vinegar, and flour.
4. Bring to boil on low heat, stir with a wooden spoon to avoid lumps (approximately it will take 30 seconds).
5. Now, add this sweet and sour sauce into the cooker and mix with the baby onions.
6. Serve immediately and enjoy the taste.

Nutritional Information

- Preparation Time: 20 minutes
- Total Servings: 2
- Calories: 168

- Calories from Fat: 106
- Fat: 11.8g
- Saturated Fat: 7.4g
- Cholesterol: 31mg
- Carbohydrates: 14.6g
- Fiber: 2.6g
- Sugar: 6.9g
- Protein: 2.4g

Tips to extra flavor

- For better taste, make a small hole in middle of the onions

Recipe 11: Mixed Vegetable Medley

Ingredients

- Eggplant 1
- Olive oil 30ml
- Medium pepper half
- Medium zucchinis 1
- Chopped onion 30g
- White radish 1
- Cherry tomatoes 5
- Capers 10g
- Pine nuts 15g
- Raisins 10g
- Olives 15g
- Basil 1 bunch
- Salt and Pepper to taste

Preparation Method

1. At first, wash and slice all vegetables. Set your instant pot cooker on sauté mode and add olive oil. When oil is hot, add onions and cook for 3 minutes.
2. After 3 minutes, add radish, eggplant, pepper, zucchini and cook for 10 minutes, occasionally stir every 2 minutes with a wooden stick.
3. Finally, add chopped raisins, basil, olives, capers, pine nuts, salt, pepper to taste and add 240ml of water. Set cooker timer for 5 minutes at high pressure.
4. When beep sounds, open the lid and add cherry tomato, fresh olive oil, vinegar and serve hot.

Nutritional Information

- Preparation Time: 20 minutes
- Total Servings: 2
- Calories: 191
- Calories from Fat: 45
- Fat: 5g
- Saturated Fat: 0.7g
- Cholesterol: 0mg
- Sodium: 257mg
- Potassium: 1022mg
- Carbohydrates: 34.6g
- Fiber: 7.5g
- Sugar: 5.5g
- Protein: 4g

Tips to extra flavor

- Add only 1 cup of water

Recipe 12: Salsa Shredded Chicken

Ingredients

- Chicken breast 250g
- Kosher salt 2g
- Cumin 2g
- Black pepper to taste
- Oregano to taste
- Chunky salsa 50g

Preparation Method

1. At first, season chicken on both sides with spices. Put in instant pot cooker and cover with salsa.
2. Select poultry option and set the timer for 20 minutes on high pressure.
3. Once the instant pot cooker releases the pressure, put the chicken onto a plate and shred the chicken using a fork. Serve hot and enjoy the taste.

Nutritional Information

- Preparation Time: 25 minutes
- Total Servings: 2
- Calories: 125
- Calories from Fat: 68
- Fat: 6g
- Saturated Fat: 2.2g
- Cholesterol: 66mg
- Sodium: 379mg
- Potassium:

- Carbohydrates: 3g
- Fiber: 1g
- Sugar: 0g
- Protein: 22g

Tips to extra flavor

- Try to put salsa only on top on chicken pieces

Recipe 13: Sweet Glazed Meatloaf

Ingredients

Meatloaf:
- Ground beef 250g
- Egg white 1
- Diced onion 40g
- Black olives 2
- Fresh basil leaves (as needed)
- Salt 1g
- Black pepper 1g
- Ketchup 14g
- Minced garlic 3g
- Ground flaxseed 5g

Glaze:
- Spicy brown mustard 8g

- Ketchup 25g

Preparation Method

1. At first, mix all ingredients except the glaze ingredients together by hand and then form a loaf in a bowl.
2. In a separate bowl, add all glaze ingredients and mix well. Pour this mixture on top of the meatloaf. Cover the bowl tightly using foil.
3. Add 240ml water to instant pot cooker and add trivet then place your meatloaf on top of the trivet. Select Meat/Stew option and set the timer for 45 minutes.
4. When the cooker beeps, release the pressure and enjoy the taste.

Nutritional Information

- Preparation Time: 50 minutes
- Total Servings: 2
- Calories: 270
- Calories from Fat:181
- Fat: 20.1g
- Saturated Fat: 7.9g
- Cholesterol: 112mg
- Carbohydrates: 24.1g
- Fiber: 0.4g
- Sugar: 11.4g
- Protein: 18.4g

Tips to extra flavor

- You can add extra ketchup before serving

Recipe 14: Fresh Berry Compote

Ingredients

- Fresh strawberries 300g
- Fresh blueberries 150g
- Lemon juice 28g
- Water 14g
- Coconut starch 10g

Preparation Method

1. At first, add sugar, blueberries, strawberries, lemon juice to the instant pot cooker and mix well.
2. Set timer for 3 minutes on high pressure and 5 minutes with natural pressure release (approximately 10 minutes).
3. On the other hand, mix coconut starch, water in a small bowl. Add this mixture to the cooking pot and select sauté mode, don't forget to stir constantly.
4. Put all this mixture jar or storage container and place in refrigerate until ready to serve on a plate.

Nutritional Information

- Preparation Time: 15 minutes
- Total Servings: 2
- Calories: 134
- Calories from Fat: 0.9
- Fat: 0.1g
- Saturated Fat: 0g
- Cholesterol: 0g

- Carbohydrates: 35g
- Fiber: 2g
- Sugar: 28.1g
- Protein: 0.3g

Tips to extra flavor

- Wait until it comes to room temperature and later refrigerate

Lunch Recipes

Recipe 15: Pork Coarse Roast

Ingredients

- Coarse black pepper 2g
- Salt 2g
- Onion powder 2g
- Garlic powder 2g
- Chili powder 2g
- Pork sirloin tip roast 350g
- Vegetable oil 14g
- Water 140ml
- Apple juice 40ml

Preparation Method

1. In a small bowl, add spices and rub that spice mixture all over pork roast.
2. Add oil to your instant pot cooker and select browning option. When oil is hot, add pork and roast until it turns to golden brown on both sides.
3. Now, add the water, apple juice to the pressure cooker pot. Close the lid and set the timer for 25 minutes.
4. When beep sounds, wait for natural press release (approximately 5 minutes) and serve hot.

Nutritional Information

- Preparation Time: 30 minutes
- Total Servings: 2

- Calories: 406
- Calories from Fat: 171
- Fat: 19g
- Saturated Fat: 8g
- Cholesterol: 92mg
- Carbohydrates: 32.6g
- Fiber: 1.4g
- Sugar: 16.2g
- Protein: 23.2g

Tips to extra flavor

- Try using a liner in your pressure cooker for easier cleanup

Recipe 16: Green Onion Chicken

Ingredients

- Chicken 900g
- Oil 14g
- Garnish: Green onions

Sauce:

- Filipino soy sauce 60ml
- Light soy sauce 100ml
- Filipino vinegar 40ml
- Fish sauce 14g
- Sugar 14g
- Crushed garlic cloves 10
- Chopped small white onion 1
- Ground black peppercorn 5g
- Red chili 1
- Bay leaves 4

Preparation Method

1. At first, mix vinegar, soy sauces (Filipino and light), fish sauce and sugar in a medium bowl.
2. Add oil to instant pot cooker on sauté mode, brown the chicken for 2 minutes when skin turns to golden color then remove the chicken from the pot and keep aside.
3. Now, sauté onion, garlic until it fragrant then, add red chili, ground black peppercorn, red chili, and bay leaves for 30 seconds. Now, add the sauce mixture.

4. Set timer for 9 minutes at high pressure with the natural pressure release.

Nutritional Information

- Preparation Time: 35 minutes
- Total Servings: 2
- Calories: 520
- Calories from Fat: 277
- Fat: 30.7g
- Saturated Fat: 8.3g
- Cholesterol: 188mg
- Carbohydrates: 2.2g
- Fiber: 0.3g
- Sugar: 0.2g
- Protein: 44.5g

Tips to extra flavor

- After opening instant pot cooker, remove all bay leaves

Recipe 17: Italian Tenderloin Pork

Ingredients

- Tenderloin pork 110g
- Olive oil 15g
- Crushed tomatoes 150g
- Roasted red peppers 50g
- Fresh thyme 3g
- Bay leaves 1
- Chopped fresh parsley 6g
- Kosher salt 2g
- Black pepper to taste

Preparation Method

1. At first, season your pork with salt and pepper to nice taste. Select sauté button and add oil, garlic and sauté until turns to golden brown (approximately 1 minute), remove using a slotted spoon.
2. Now, add pork and cook until it turns brown on each side (about 2 minutes). Add the remaining all ingredients but reserve half of the parsley for garnish.
3. Set cooker at high pressure for 45 minutes, wait for the natural release. When it finished, remove bay leaves, shred the pork using forks and top with remaining parsley. Serve over your favorite pasta.

Nutritional Information

- Preparation Time: 55 minutes
- Total Servings: 2
- Calories: 93

- Calories from Fat: 34
- Fat:1.5g
- Saturated Fat: 0.5g
- Cholesterol: 33mg
- Carbohydrates: 6.5g
- Fiber: 0g
- Sugar: 3g
- Protein: 11g

Tips to extra flavor

- If desire, eat with salad. It creates extra yummy taste to mouth

Recipe 18: Yummy Barbecue Beef

Ingredients

- Garlic 2 cloves
- Chopped onion half
- Lime juice 10ml
- Chipotles 26g (mixed in adobo sauce)
- Ground cumin 7g
- Ground oregano 7g
- Ground cloves 1g
- Water 150ml
- Beef 350g (bottom roast)
- Salt 2g
- Black pepper to taste
- Oil 5g
- Bay leaves 1

Preparation Method

1. At first, put your ingredients like onion, garlic, cloves, cumin, lime juice, oregano, chipotles and water in a mixer and make a thick paste out of it.
2. On the other hand, trim all the fat off meat and your beef into 3-inch pieces. Season with salt and black pepper for subtle, delicious taste. Select sauté button on the cooker; add oil and slowly add beef pieces and brown all sides, approximately 5 minutes.

3. Add the paste and bay leave in the pot and set the cooking timer to 65 minutes on the high pressure until the meat is tender and easily shreds with a fork.
4. Once it is done, remove the bay leaf and add salt, cumin and enjoy the taste.

Nutritional Information

- Preparation Time: 80 minutes
- Total Servings: 2
- Calories: 153
- Calories from Fat: 65
- Fat: 4.5g
- Saturated Fat: 2.3g
- Cholesterol: 44mg
- Carbohydrates: 2g
- Sugar: 0g
- Protein: 24g

Tips to extra flavor

- For luscious taste, garnish with chopped red onions, cilantro, lime pieces before serving

Recipe 19: Lime Chicken Sauce

Ingredients

- Chicken thighs 450g (skinless and boneless)
- Lime juice 15ml
- Fish sauce 5g
- Olive oil 15g
- Coconut milk 14g
- Grated fresh ginger 7g
- Fresh mint 7g
- Fresh cilantro 14g

Preparation Method

1. At first, rinse your chicken breasts and trim any excess fat. Put in bottom of the instant pot cooker.
2. In a mason jar, combine all remaining ingredients and shake well. Add this mixture to the chicken.
3. Select poultry option in your instant pot setting and reduce time to 10 minutes.
4. Use the quick release lid setting when done. Drain excess liquid and enjoy the taste.

Nutritional Information

- Preparation Time: 20 minutes
- Total Servings: 2
- Calories: 220
- Calories from Fat:96
- Fat:10.7g

- Saturated Fat: 4.5g
- Cholesterol: 84mg
- Sodium: 555mg
- Potassium: 341mg
- Carbohydrates: 2.6g
- Fiber: 0.3g
- Sugar: 0.6g
- Protein: 27.7g

Tips to extra flavor

- Before serving, add fresh chopped basil leaves for extra taste

Recipe 20: Barbeque Chicken Curry

Ingredients

- Chicken thighs 200g (skinless and boneless)
- Ground paprika 2g
- Salt and pepper to taste
- Minced onion 30g
- Water 70ml
- Chile or hot sauce 20ml
- Vinegar 10g

Preparation Method

1. At first, heat your instant pot cooker over medium heat and cook chicken until browned approximately 10 minutes. Sprinkle salt, pepper, and paprika on chicken for extra taste.
2. In a separate bowl, add water, vinegar, onion, hot sauce and mix until it combines well with sauce. Add this sauce to chicken.
3. Close pot and set timer for 15 minutes with natural release.
4. If desired, add chopped herbs over it for extra delicious taste.

Nutritional Information

- Preparation Time: 25 minutes
- Total Servings: 2
- Calories: 218
- Calories from Fat: 107
- Fat: 11.9
- Saturated Fat: 3.3

- Cholesterol: 71
- Carbohydrates: 7
- Fiber: 0.8
- Sugar: 3.1
- Protein: 19.8

Tips to extra flavor

- Make sure that you cook chicken for long enough, to avoid too watery curry

Recipe 21: Mixed Pepper Salad

Ingredients

- Red peppers 1
- Yellow peppers 1
- Green pepper half
- Sliced tomatoes 1
- Red Onion 30g
- Garlic 1 clove
- Fresh parsley 12g
- Olive oil 7g
- Salt and pepper to taste

Preparation Method

1. At first, wash and remove the stems and seeds from the peppers. Slice the peppers into thin strips and chop the tomatoes into small pieces.
2. Put your instant pot cooker in sauté mode and add oil and red onions. When onions begin to soften, add garlic, clove, and peppers without stirring, let one side of the pepper turn brown (approximately 5 minutes).
3. Now, add the tomato puree, salt, and pepper, mix well until it mixed well. Set cooker cooking time to 6 minutes at high pressure on natural release.
4. Before serving, add one raw clove, smashed garlic, freshly chopped basil and served hot.

Nutritional Information

- Preparation Time: 10 minutes
- Total Servings: 2

- Calories: 196
- Calories from Fat: 87
- Fat: 9.6g
- Saturated Fat: 1.5g
- Cholesterol: 0mg
- Carbohydrates: 28.6g
- Fiber: 3.7g
- Sugar: 7.7g
- Protein: 4g

Tips to extra flavor

- For extra taste, add ghee roasted garlic and ginger

Recipe 22: Chicken Okra Soup

Ingredients

- Coconut milk 120g
- Water 300g
- Curry sauce mix 1 portions
- Ground ginger 2g
- Broccoli paste 55g
- Carrots paste 55g
- Water chestnut 55g
- Frozen okra 85g
- Cooked chicken breast 8g

Preparation Method

1. Place all ingredients in instant pot cooker and select soup option.
2. That it's after a few minutes your tasty soup will be ready.

Nutritional Information

- Preparation Time: 20 minutes
- Total Servings: 2
- Calories: 179
- Calories from Fat: 39
- Fat: 4.4g
- Saturated Fat: 0.7g
- Cholesterol: 0mg
- Carbohydrates: 32.2g
- Fiber: 6.5g

- Sugar: 5.1g
- Protein: 4.4g

Tips to extra flavor

- If desired, add chopped cilantro, basil on top before serving

Recipe 23: Ground Kale Soup

Ingredients

- Chopped onion 40g
- Kale 80g
- Almond milk 28g
- Ground garlic 5g
- Ground sausage 80g
- Thyme 10g
- Chicken stock 100ml
- Red pepper and salt to taste

Preparation Method

1. At first, set your instant pot cooker to sauté mode and add onion, garlic, and ground sausage.
2. After 3 minutes, add potatoes and seasoning (like thyme, salt, red pepper) and chicken stock, stir well.
3. Select soup option and set the timer for 25 minutes. After that, open lid and add chopped kale, almond milk on sauté mode.
4. Before serving, top with a little parsley. It tastes great next day also.

Nutritional Information

- Preparation Time: 30 minutes
- Total Servings: 2
- Calories: 266
- Calories from Fat: 155
- Fat: 17g

- Saturated Fat: 8.1g
- Cholesterol: 45mg
- Carbohydrates: 16.1g
- Fiber: 1.5g
- Sugar: 3.1g
- Protein: 10.6g

Tips to extra flavor

- Don't sauté kale more and add chopped parsley before serving

Recipe 24: Vegetable Duck

Ingredients

- Duck (small size)
- Sliced cucumber half
- Sliced carrots 1
- Cooking wine 7g
- Water 250g
- 1-inch ginger piece
- Salt 10g

Preparation Method

1. Put all ingredients into the instant cooker pot and then press the stew option. Within a few minutes, the delicious soup will be ready in no time.

Nutritional Information

- Preparation Time: 40 minutes
- Total Servings: 2
- Calories: 199
- Calories from Fat: 64
- Fat: 2.9g
- Saturated Fat: 0.9g
- Cholesterol: 55mg
- Carbohydrates: 29.3g
- Fiber: 4.1g
- Sugar: 2.7g
- Protein: 19.3g

Tips to extra flavor

- Before serving, sprinkle little pepper on top

Recipe 25: Mushroom Broth Soup

Ingredients

- Vegetable oil 14g
- Mushrooms 12g
- Beef broth 30ml
- Water 300ml
- Coconut milk 30ml
- Coconut flour 25g

Preparation Method

1. At first, add oil to instant pot cooker and press sauté button. Add sliced mushroom, beef broth and cook until mushrooms turn to golden color.
2. Now, add water and select pressurize mode with a quick release. Drain broth and mushroom and reserve broth. Place mushrooms back.
3. Add butter and coconut flour to a saucepan, stir until it smells like pie crust.
4. Now, add broth until it forms texture. Add milk and continue to whisk occasionally on simmer for approximately 8 minutes.
5. Pour into a bowl and enjoy creamy mushroom soup.

Nutritional Information

- Preparation Time: 25 minutes
- Total Servings: 2
- Calories: 278
- Calories from Fat: 116
- Fat: 6.8g
- Saturated Fat: 1.9g

- Cholesterol: 95mg
- Carbohydrates: 24.1g
- Fiber: 1.6g
- Sugar: 3.7g
- Protein: 14g

Tips to extra flavor

- Coconut flour can be replaced almond starch for better taste

Recipe 26: Indian Style Goat Meat

Ingredients

- Fresh goat meat 300g
- Garlic 4 cloves
- Small chopped onions 1
- Medium shallot 1
- Ginger 10g
- Medium white radish
- Cilantro 10g
- Olive oil 28g
- Curry powder 30g
- Chili powder 3g
- Tomato paste 100ml
- Water 250ml
- Salt and black pepper to taste

Preparation Method

1. At first, select sauté button and add 14g of olive oil into the cooker pot.
2. Add your goat meat into the cooker. Add kosher salt and black pepper to taste. Cook for 5 minutes and set aside.
3. Again, add 14g of olive oil into the cooker and add sliced onion, minced ginger, garlic, and shallot, then stir for a minute (until fragrant nicely).
4. Add curry powder and Indian chili pepper to the pot and stir 2 minutes. Add the water to the cooker.
5. Put goat meat in the cooker and add tomato paste on top of the goat meat. Do not stir. Add radish and set instant pot cooker at high pressure for 35 to 40

minutes. Turn off the heat and wait for natural release (approximately 15 minutes).
6. Garnish with chopped cilantro. Serve immediately.

Nutritional Information

- Preparation Time: 80 minutes
- Total Servings: 2
- Calories: 256
- Calories from Fat: 91
- Total Fat: 10.1g
- Saturated Fat: 2g
- Cholesterol: 66mg
- Carbohydrates: 13.2g
- Fiber: 1.9g
- Sugar: 2.2g
- Protein: 22.8g

Tips to extra flavor

For delicious taste, try to eat with basmati rice or flatbread called naan or chapatti or roti

Recipe 27: Tasty Pineapple Spare Ribs

Ingredients

- Olive oil 14g
- Ribs 600g
- Medium onion 1
- Ketchup 30g
- Soy sauce 15ml
- Rice wine vinegar 15ml
- Pineapple 220g
- Garlic 2 cloves
- Chopped ginger 3g
- Fish sauce 3g
- Chili powder 3g
- Ground coriander 3g
- Smoked paprika to taste
- Salt and pepper to taste

Preparation Method

1. At first, add oil to instant pot cooker and sauté onions until just translucent. Add all ingredients except coconut starch slurry. Make sure that spareribs are submerged in sauce.
2. Put your cooker on stew mode for 12 minutes, leave on keeping warm for 3 minutes and wait for natural pressure release. Check meat for doneness and moisture. If needed more time set the timer to stew mode for a few more minutes.

3. When meat is done, remove meat to a bowl and add your favorite seasonings for extra taste (if needed). Select sauté and let sauce starts to boil, add coconut starch slurry to thicken the sauce for extra delicious taste.
4. Serve with rice and veggies based on your choice.

Nutritional Information

- Preparation Time: 25 minutes
- Total Servings: 2
- Calories: 668
- Calories from Fat: 303
- Fat: 33.7g
- Saturated Fat: 11.6g
- Cholesterol: 120mg
- Carbohydrates: 59.1g
- Fiber: 0.6g
- Sugar: 44g
- Protein: 31.9g

Tips to extra flavor

- Coconut starch helps to thicken the sauce and increase the taste

Recipe 28: Butter Coconut Chicken

Ingredients

- Chicken thighs 4 pieces (skinless)
- Diced tomatoes 200g
- Jalapeno peppers 1
- Fresh ginger root 10g
- Vegetable butter 45ml
- Ground cumin 5g
- Paprika 10g
- Kosher salt 5g
- Coconut cream 40g
- Almond yogurt 40g
- Garam masala 5g
- Roasted cumin seeds 5g
- Coconut starch 10g
- Water 15ml
- Cilantro 10g

Preparation Method

1. At first, blend your tomatoes, jalapeno, and ginger to paste and puree.
2. Add butter to instant cooking pot, select browning option. When butter is hot, add the chicken pieces, a few at a time, and char until they are nicely browned all sides. Remove them using slotted spoon and put aside.
3. Now, add ground cumin and paprika to the butter pot and cook for 10-15 seconds, then add the tomato mixture, salt, almond yogurt, coconut cream and

roasted chicken pieces to the pot. Gently stir the chicken pieces to coat the nicely. Close the lid and select 5 minutes cook time.
4. When the timer beeps, wait for natural pressure release (around 10 minutes). When you open the lid, immediately add garam masala and roasted cumin.
5. Now, in a separate small bowl, whisk coconut starch and stir into the pot.
6. Select sauté and bring to a boil for 2 minutes and add minced cilantro. Serve hot.

Nutritional Information

- Preparation Time: 60 minutes
- Total Servings: 2
- Calories: 880
- Calories from Fat: 741
- Fat: 81.1g
- Saturated Fat: 32.1g
- Cholesterol: 303mg
- Sodium: 1461mg
- Potassium: 567mg
- Carbohydrates: 12.8g
- Fiber: 2.6g
- Sugar: 4.6g
- Protein: 26.4g

Tips to extra flavor

- Don't forget to add coconut starch; it will thicken your sauce in chicken

Recipe 29: Pepper Chicken Curry

Ingredients

- Olive oil 14g
- Chicken thighs 300g
- Large onion 1
- Garlic 2 cloves
- Dried oregano 2g
- Red pepper flakes 2g
- Bay leaf 1
- Diced tomatoes 300g
- Chicken broth 30ml
- Green bell peppers 1
- Salt and pepper to taste

Preparation Method

1. Heat olive oil in an instant pot cooker by selecting a brown option. Sprinkle chicken with salt and pepper and cook the chicken until it turns to golden brown color, about 5 minutes, add more olive oil if necessary. Transfer chicken to plate.
2. Add onion to the cooker, select sauté mode and cook onion until soft, scraping up browned bits, about 4 minutes. Add garlic, red pepper flakes, oregano and cook until fragrant (around 1 minute).
3. Add chicken broth, bay leaf, tomatoes and chicken to cooker. Close and set cooking time for 10 minutes. When it is finished, open lid; add green peppers and stir until mixed well in the mixture. Close lid once again and increase cooking time to 2 more minutes, select quick release.
4. Remove bay leaf. Season with salt and pepper. Serve over rice or pasta.

Nutritional Information

- Preparation Time: 30 minutes
- Total Servings: 2
- Calories: 321
- Calories from Fat: 112
- Fat: 12.4g
- Saturated Fat: 2.8g
- Cholesterol: 69mg
- Carbohydrates: 13.3g
- Fiber: 2.6g
- Sugar: 7.6g
- Protein: 22.2g

Tips to extra flavor

- Don't forget to remove the bay leaf before serving

Recipe 30: Boiled Sweet Potatoes

Ingredients

- Large sweet potatoes 2
- Water 120ml
- Topping: Extra virgin olive oil

Preparation Method

1. Scour your potatoes, apply olive oil and wrap in aluminum foil. Add 120ml of water in instant pot cooker and add potatoes.
2. Press the steam button and set time to 15 minutes. Remove foil, cut a slit in the top of sweet potatoes and enjoy.
3. Top with your favorite nuts like walnuts, ground flax seeds, etc.
4. If a kid is eating, 3-4 miniature marshmallows on warm, sweet potatoes go over big.

Nutritional Information

- Preparation Time: 20 minutes
- Total Servings: 2
- Calories: 180
- Calories from Fat:
- Fat: 0.4g
- Saturated Fat: 0g
- Cholesterol: 0mg
- Carbohydrates: 42g
- Fiber: 3.3g
- Sugar: 6g

- Protein: 4g

Tips to extra flavor

- Make small and thin scratch over sweet potatoes before cooking

Recipe31: Pumpkin Puree

Ingredients

- Medium sugar pumpkin 1

Preparation Method

1. Add 80ml of water to your instant pot cooker. Place the pumpkin on the rack and cook on high pressure for 15 minutes. Select quick release and set aside for a few minutes to cool.
2. Scoop flesh out of pumpkin into a bowl and make a paste using a hand blender or with an immersion blender and you can serve with your favorite herb sauce.

Nutritional Information

- Preparation Time: minutes
- Total Servings: 2
- Calories: 189
- Calories from Fat: 7g
- Fat: 0.7g
- Saturated Fat: 0.4g
- Cholesterol: 0mg
- Carbohydrates: 47.2g
- Fiber: 3.6g
- Sugar: 9.9g
- Protein: 7.3g

Tips to extra flavor

- Before cooking, wash and remove skin of the pumpkin

Dinner Recipes

Recipe 32: Vinegar Chicken

Ingredients

- Chicken thighs 600g
- White vinegar 15g
- Fish sauce 10g
- Garlic 2 cloves
- Black peppercorns 2g
- Bay leaves 2

Preparation Method

1. Select poultry option in your instant pot cooker and add chicken including your ingredients (you don't have to sauté anything).
2. Close the lid, and cook for 15 minutes. Serve hot.

Nutritional Information

- Preparation Time: 20 minutes
- Total Servings: 2
- Calories: 544
- Calories from Fat: 272
- Fat: 30.2g
- Saturated Fat: 6.7g
- Cholesterol: 142mg
- Carbohydrates: 26.6g
- Fiber: 0.8g

- Sugar: 22g
- Protein: 38.9g

Tips to extra flavor

- Before serving, sprinkle with dry basil leaves and dry oregano

Recipe 33: Chicken Cola Wings

Ingredients

- Chicken wings 300g
- Garlic 2 cloves
- Green onion 1 stalk
- Sliced ginger 14g
- Coca Cola 100g
- Light soy sauce 14g
- Dark soy sauce 7g
- Rice wine 7g
- Vegetable oil 7g

Preparation Method

1. At first, select sauté mode in your instant pot cooker and add oil.
2. When oil is hot, add ginger, garlic, onions and sauté until fragrant nicely.
3. Now, add slowly chicken wings and stir approximately 2minutes or until wings are coated all sides with gravy.
4. When edges of wings turn to golden brown and immediately add coca cola, stir using a wooden spoon and add both soy sauce (dark and light), rice wine. Mix well until it combined well and select cooker cooking timer for 5 minutes on high pressure and wait for natural pressure release (approximately 10 minutes).
5. If desired, add extra seasoning (it shouldn't taste like coca cola). Serve immediately with rice or brown rice.

Nutritional Information

- Preparation Time: 30 minutes
- Total Servings: 2

- Calories: 280
- Calories from Fat: 115
- Fat: 14.1g
- Saturated Fat: 3.1g
- Cholesterol: 78mg
- Carbohydrates: 14.2g
- Fiber: 0g
- Sugar: 12.8g
- Protein: 19g

Tips to extra flavor

- Serve with your favorite dish

Recipe 34: Hot Honey Drumstick

Ingredients

- Soy sauce 25ml
- Rice wine 20ml
- Honey 14g
- Garlic 2 cloves
- Fresh grated ginger 2g
- Sriracha hot sauce 3g
- Chicken drumsticks 4 pieces
- Sesame seeds 7g
- Chopped scallions 5g

Preparation Method

1. At first, select the sauté option in your instant pot cooker and add garlic, ginger, honey, rice wine, soy sauce, sriracha sauce and cook for 2 minutes.
2. Now, add the chicken and set the cooking timer to 20 minutes on the high pressure until the chicken is tender. When pressure is released naturally, add finely chopped scallions and sesame seeds over it and serve.

Nutritional Information

- Preparation Time: 55 minutes
- Total Servings: 2
- Calories: 309
- Calories from Fat: 160
- Fat: 7.5g
- Saturated Fat: 2.1g

- Cholesterol: 152mg
- Carbohydrates: 22g
- Fiber: 0.5g
- Sugar: 18.5g
- Protein: 34.5g

Tips to extra flavor

- Before serving, add roasted sesame seeds on top for extra taste

Recipe 35: Salt Roasted Chicken

Ingredients

- Chicken legs 4 pieces
- Dried ground ginger 5g
- Kosher salt 4g
- Five spice powder 2g
- Optional: Ground white pepper 3g
- Water 120ml

Preparation Method

1. At first, place the chicken legs in a large mixing bowl and season with dried ginger, five spice powder, kosher salt and mix well until the chicken legs are coated well (for better taste make a small scratch over legs)
2. Wrap the chicken legs tightly in a large piece of parchment paper (avoid aluminum foil).
3. Put a steamer rack in the instant pot cooker and add 240ml of water. Carefully place the chicken legs on the rack. Close the lid and set the timer for 25 minutes on high pressure with natural pressure release (natural pressure release takes approximately 20 minutes).
4. When it is done, unwrap the parchment paper carefully and serve immediately.

Nutritional Information

- Preparation Time: 50 minutes
- Total Servings: 2
- Calories: 483
- Calories from Fat:172

- Fat: 19.2g
- Saturated Fat: 5.1g
- Cholesterol: 55mg
- Carbohydrates: 48.6g
- Fiber: 5.2g
- Sugar: 0g
- Protein: 19.1g

Tips to extra flavor

- Before serving, add black pepper on top for extra flavor

Ingredients

- Turkey thighs 1 pieces
- Chicken broth 120ml
- Red-wine vinegar 7g
- Sliced onions 75g
- Portobello mushrooms 60g
- Minced garlic 5g
- 1g each dried rosemary, sage, thyme, salt and pepper

Preparation Method

1. At first, set your instant pot cooker on sauté mode and brown the turkey thighs. Next, add all your ingredients and select poultry option and set the timer for 60 minutes.
2. When it is finished, separate the turkey pieces from gravy and cover loosely with foil.
3. In a small bowl, mix cornflour and water until well mixed and add this liquid to the gravy.
4. Select keep warm option and cook gravy for 15 minutes or until gravy thickened.
5. Before serving, add this gravy over the turkey and enjoy the delicious taste.

Nutritional Information

- Preparation Time: 35 minutes
- Total Servings: 2
- Calories: 506
- Calories from Fat: 156
- Fat: 17.4g
- Saturated Fat: 4.8g
- Cholesterol: 178mg
- Sodium: 693mg
- Potassium: 847mg
- Carbohydrates: 9.6g
- Fiber: 1.8g
- Sugar: 3.6g
- Protein: 18.7g

Tips to extra flavor

- If you want a dry curry then increase the cooking time or if you want more gravy than decrease the cooking time

Recipe 37: Barbeque Pork

Ingredients

- Pork butt roast 300g
- Garlic powder 2g
- Salt and Pepper to taste
- Barbecue sauce 40g

Preparation Method

1. At first, season the pork with salt, pepper and garlic powder.
2. Place this seasoned pork into instant pot cooker and fill enough water until pork covers.
3. Close the pot and set the timer for 60 minutes with the natural pressure release.
4. After a natural pressure release, separate juices from the meat.
5. Now, shred the pork and mix with barbecue sauce, add reserved juice if needed to reach your desired consistency.

Nutritional Information

- Preparation Time: 65 minutes
- Total Servings: 2
- Calories: 353
- Calories from Fat: 192
- Fat: 21.3
- Saturated Fat: 7.8
- Cholesterol: 89
- Carbohydrates: 15.4
- Fiber: 0.3

- Sugar: 11
- Protein: 23.1

Tips to extra flavor

- Aluminum foil can be used to keep food moist, cook it evenly, and make cleanup easier.

Recipe 38: Bell Kabadiya Sausage

Ingredients

- Olive oil 28g
- Chicken breasts and thighs 150g
- Prawns 50g
- Red onions 50g
- Bell peppers 50g (mixed colors)
- Garlic 14g
- Ginger 14g
- Chicken stock 200g
- Tomatoes 70g
- Creole seasoning 7g
- Worcestershire sauce 7g
- Andouille sausage 90g (pre-cooked and sliced)

Preparation Method

1. At first, set your instant pot cooker on sauté mode. Add chicken with creole seasoning and brown until all sides coated with golden color and keep aside.
2. Now, add onions, garlic, peppers and sauté until translucent. Add rice, and sauce and mix for 2 minutes.
3. Finally, add chicken, tomato puree, Worcestershire and close the lid and press rice option.
4. When the rice is cooked, release steam and add sausage and prawns. Place lid back on the pressure cooker and set timer again for 2 minutes.

Nutritional Information

- Preparation Time: 20 minutes
- Total Servings: 2
- Calories: 348
- Calories from Fat: 124
- Fat: 13.8g
- Saturated Fat: 4.5g
- Cholesterol: 72mg
- Carbohydrates: 32.3g
- Fiber: 2.2g
- Sugar: 1.4g
- Protein: 22.1g

Tips to extra flavor

- Add and stir prawns before serving

Recipe 39: Chile Posole Beer

Ingredients

- Frozen posole 450g
- Lean boneless pork 400g
- Chopped onion 50g
- Garlic 3g
- Cumin 1g
- Chicken broth/stock 2 cups
- Ground chile 15g
- Beer ½ bottle
- Mexican oregano 7g
- Bay leaves 1
- Sea salt 2g
- Fresh ground pepper

Garnish:
- Cilantro, lime, queso fresco, avocado

Preparation Method

1. At first, add the posole to the instant pot cooker and fill water to the maximum line. Select beans mode and wait for natural release (approximately 5 minutes).
2. Now, drain posole, and set aside (tender but firm).
3. Set your cooker in browning mode and brown your pork cubes, including chopped garlic, onions, cumin.
4. In a separate bowl, add red chili powder, chicken broth, beer, oregano, bay leaf, salt, pepper and mix well and add the mixture to the pot.
5. Select stew option. While the pork is cooking, try to prepare for garnishes.

6. When the timer beeps, add the posole into the pot with the tender pork. Stir once and pour into the serving bowl, and top with preferred garnishes.

Nutritional Information

- Preparation Time: 25 minutes
- Total Servings: 2
- Calories: 321
- Calories from Fat: 92
- Fat: 10.6g
- Saturated Fat: 2.7g
- Carbohydrates: 31.8g
- Fiber: 5.5g
- Sugar: 5.7g
- Protein: 15.4g

Tips to extra flavor

- Before serving, garnish with freshly chopped parsley and cilantro

Recipe 40: Vegan Chickpea Curry

Ingredients

- Olive oil 10ml
- Cumin seeds 5g
- Onion 30g
- Crushed garlic 5g
- Ground coriander 5g
- Garam masala 2g
- Ground turmeric 2g
- Cooked chickpeas 120g
- Diced tomatoes 100g
- Potatoes 25g
- Salt and pepper to taste
- Water 100ml

Garnish:

- Cilantro, parsley

Preparation Method

- At first, add oil to your instant pot cooker on saute mode, add cumin seeds. When it starts to crackle, add the sliced onion and cook for 5 minutes, when onions turns to golden color, add garlic and all remaining ingredients (except garnish).
- Close the lid and set timer for 15 minutes, when it releases pressure naturally, open and add cilantro and parsley.
- Serve with basmati rice, naan or pappadums for better taste.

Nutritional Information

- Preparation Time: 25 minutes
- Total Servings: 2
- Calories: 384.2
- Calories from Fat: 74
- Fat: 8.3g
- Saturated Fat: 1.1g
- Carbohydrates: 68.9g
- Fiber: 12g
- Sugar: 6g
- Protein: 11.6g

Tips to extra flavor

Before serving, garnish with freshly chopped parsley and cilantro for extra taste

Recipe 41: Green Chicken Thighs

Ingredients

- Chicken thighs 220g
- Fresh cilantro 14g
- Minced garlic 4g
- Minced ginger 3g
- Salt 2g
- Pepper 2g
- Minced green onion 15g
- Garlic powder 2g
- Olive oil 14g
- Balsamic Vinegar 12g
- Worcestershire sauce 3g

Preparation Method

1. At first, take one plastic bag and add salt, pepper, garlic, minced onions, Worcestershire sauce and balsamic vinegar.
2. Then add chicken to the mixture, make sure that chicken nicely covered in sauce and set aside.
3. Now, select sauté and add olive oil, minced garlic and stirring frequently.
4. Select poultry mode in your instant pot cooker and add chicken sauce bag mixture in olive oil and garlic mixture. Wait for natural release.
5. While serving, sprinkle chopped cilantro for extra taste. You can also serve with your favorite vegetable mix.

Nutritional Information

- Preparation Time: 30 minutes
- Total Servings: 2
- Calories: 238
- Calories from Fat: 110
- Fat: 12.2g
- Saturated Fat: 3.4g
- Cholesterol: 72mg
- Carbohydrates: 10.8g
- Fiber: 2.6g
- Sugar: 4g
- Protein: 20.6g

Tips to extra flavor

- Before serving, sprinkle with freshly chopped parsley

Recipe 42 Coconut Meatloaf

Ingredients

- Ground meat 450g
- Chopped onion 1
- Egg 1
- Carrot 10 pieces
- Coconut milk 240ml
- Horseradish 1-inch piece
- Sea salt to taste
- Dry garlic to taste

Topping:

- Ketchup 150g

Preparation Method

1. At first, spray cooker pot with non-stick spray. Mix all meatloaf ingredients, makes perfect round shaped loaf and place in the cooker pot.
2. Now, add radish slices around the meatloaf or next to the meatloaf.
3. Close the lid and select slow cook option and adjust the timer to 8 hours).

Nutritional Information

- Preparation Time: 6-8 hours
- Total Servings: 2
- Calories: 665
- Calories from Fat: 357
- Fat: 30.4g

- Saturated Fat: 14.9g
- Cholesterol: 223mg
- Carbohydrates: 26.2g
- Fiber: 2g
- Sugar: 6.2g
- Protein: 32.6g

Tips to extra flavor

- Aluminum foil can be used to keep food moist, cook it evenly, and make cleanup easier

Recipe 43: Red Borscht Soup

Ingredients

- Large beets 1
- Carrots 1
- Sweet potatoes 1
- Vegetable oil 7g
- Chopped onion 40g
- Fresh dill to taste
- Water with beef bouillon powder
- Sauerkraut 225g
- Fresh shredded cabbage 30g
- Fresh tomatoes 100g
- Garlic 2 cloves
- Salt and pepper to taste
- Red wine vinegar 7g
- Garnish: Fresh parsley

Preparation Method

1. At first, place your beets, sweet potatoes on steaming rack on instant pot cooker and 350ml of water and cook beets for about 30 minutes. When it is ready, dice the beets, sweet potatoes and cut into one-inch pieces.
2. After cleaning your cooking pot, select sauté option and add oil. When the oil is hot, add onions, salt, pepper, dill, parsley and cook until translucent.
3. Now, add sliced beets, sweet potatoes, carrots, sauerkraut, garlic, tomatoes to pot. Depending on your soup consistency, add water as you like.

4. Now, add sugar, ketchup, wine vinegar and mix well. Select cooking timer for 10 minutes.
5. Let pressure release naturally. Scoop the vegetables into a bowl, top with coconut cream, fresh parsley and enjoy the taste.

Nutritional Information

- Preparation Time: 45 minutes
- Total Servings: 2
- Calories: 299
- Calories from Fat: 148
- Fat: 12.5g
- Saturated Fat: 4.8g
- Cholesterol: 41mg
- Carbohydrates: 28.2g
- Fiber: 5.5g
- Sugar: 9.8g
- Protein: 14.1g

Tips to extra flavor

- Don't forget to add sour coconut cream and parsley as a topping

Recipe 44: Leafy Spinach Soup

Ingredients

- Chopped bacon slices 2
- Chopped onion 40g
- Chopped carrot 20g
- Chopped celery stalk 1
- Tomato paste 15g
- Chicken broth 2cups
- Bay leaves 1
- Fresh rosemary 1 spring
- Fresh baby spinach 1 cups

Preparation Method

1. At first, blend the beans with 240ml water using mixer or blender.
2. Select sauté option and cook bacon until it becomes crispy. Set aside.
3. Now, add the onion, celery, and carrots to the pot and cook until it becomes soft (approximately 5 minutes). After that add tomato paste and bean paste, rosemary and bay leave.
4. Set cooker timer for 15 minutes on high pressure. Let the pressure release naturally, before serving before rosemary and bay leaves.
5. To serve, ladle into 6 bowls and top with crispy bacon slices.

Nutritional Information

- Preparation Time: 20 minutes
- Total Servings: 2 cups
- Calories: 211

- Calories from Fat: 110
- Fat: 1.5g
- Saturated Fat: 0.5g
- Cholesterol: 2mg
- Carbohydrates: 39g
- Fiber: 12g
- Sugar: 4g
- Protein: 15g

Tips to extra flavor

- Add spinach at the end and top with chopped bacon

Recipe 45: Vegetable Spice Soup

Ingredients

- Celery 115g
- Carrots 12g
- Chopped onion 40g
- Fresh jalapeno half
- Olive oil 14g
- Coriander seeds 3g
- Cumin seed 2g
- Chicken broth 14g
- Water 2 cups
- Ground turmeric 2g
- Ground cumin 3g
- Optional: chopped cilantro

Preparation Method

1. At first, set your instant pot cooker on sauté mode and add olive oil to the pot.
2. When oil is hot, add coriander seeds and cumin seeds and wait until the coriander seeds pop. Now, add chopped onions, jalapeno, celery, and carrots.
3. Sauté until the onions become translucent, approximately 5 minutes. Now, add the turmeric, pickled jalapenos and cumin. Once it releases nice aroma, add potatoes and chicken broth.
4. Set cooker mode to soup and set timer for 30 minutes. Let pressure release normally and before serving, add chopped cilantro for an excellent taste. You can have with bread slices.

Nutritional Information

- Preparation Time: 35 minutes
- Total Servings: 2
- Calories: 155
- Calories from Fat:101
- Fat: 11.2g
- Saturated Fat: 4.9g
- Cholesterol: 27mg
- Carbohydrates: 9.9g
- Fiber: 2.7g
- Sugar: 3.4g
- Protein: 5.4g

Tips to extra flavor

- Right before you serve, add freshly chopped cilantro and basil for extra flavor and taste

Recipe 46: Red Cabbage Salad

Ingredients

- Red cabbage 200g
- Chopped onion 40g
- Granny smith apple 1
- Red wine vinegar 20ml
- Dry red wine 60g
- Bay leaves 2
- Beef broth 120ml
- Salt 5g
- Ground cloves 2g
- Cinnamon ½ stick
- Coconut flour 7g

Preparation Method

1. At first, using a hand blender with slicing disk; blend the cabbage and keep aside.
2. Set your instant pot cooker on sauté mode and add butter. When butter is hot, add onion, apple and sauté until it becomes soft (approximately 10 minutes).
3. Now, add the cabbage, salt, cinnamon stick, vinegar, cloves, bay leaves, broth, coconut flour and gently stir to avoid lumps.
4. Select a manual option and set the timer for 10 minutes. After that again, press sauté option and bring to a boil for 5 minutes or until it becomes thick.

Nutritional Information

- Preparation Time: 30 minutes

- Total Servings: 2
- Calories: 120
- Calories from Fat: 33
- Fat: 3.7g
- Saturated Fat: 0.5g
- Cholesterol: 0mg
- Carbohydrates: 22.4g
- Fiber: 3.2g
- Sugar: 15.5g
- Protein: 1.8g

Tips to extra flavor

- It should not be blended more, and it is a traditional favorite for a German feast

Recipe 47: Tasty Fruit Soup

Ingredients

- Cantaloupe half
- Small orange 1
- Peaches 1
- Pineapple juice 220ml
- Plain almond yogurt 110g
- Vanilla extract 2g
- Powdered sugar 7g
- Chia seeds 7g

Preparation Method

1. At first, add fruit and pineapple juice to instant pot cooker.
2. Set cooker time for 5 minutes on high pressure with quick release mode, when time up.
3. Use an immersion blender; blend until it becomes completely smooth. Using a strainer, remove any bulky pulp.
4. When it becomes cold, add almond yogurt, sugar, vanilla and mix well until it looks smooth.
5. Place it in the refrigerator and serve cold with extra yogurt and little chia seeds.

Nutritional Information

- Preparation Time:15 minutes
- Total Servings: 2
- Calories: 96
- Calories from Fat: 3

- Fat: 0.3g
- Saturated Fat: 0.1g
- Cholesterol: 0mg
- Carbohydrates: 16.4g
- Fiber: 1g
- Sugar: 12.6g
- Protein: 1.8g

Tips to extra flavor

- Using a spoon, carefully remove pulp from cantaloupe

Recipe 48: Anise Chicken Honey

Ingredients

- Chicken wings 380g
- Garlic cloves 2
- Onion 30g
- Star anise 1
- Ginger 10g
- Honey 10g
- Warm water 100ml
- Almond oil 10g
- Coconut starch 14g

Chicken Wing Marinade:

- Light fish sauce 14g
- Dark fish sauce 10g
- Shaoxing wine 10g
- Raw honey 2g
- Salt 2g

Preparation Method

1. At first, marinate the chicken wings by mixing all chicken wing marinade ingredients and keep aside for 20 minutes.
2. Select sauté option. When the pot is hot, add almond oil into the pot. This will help to prevent the chicken wings from sticking to the pot.
3. Now, add marinated chicken wings into the pot, brown the chicken wings for 30 seconds on each side or until it turns to golden color. If necessary, flip for few times because the fish sauce and honey can be burnt easily. Remove and set aside.

4. Sauté the onions, ginger, garlic, star anise, honey with 120ml warm water.
5. Finally, add all the chicken wings with all the meat juice and the leftover chicken wing marinade into the cooker pot and set the timer for 5 minutes on high pressure.
6. When it finishes, open the lid and taste sauce. F desired, add more salt or honey.
7. In separate small bowl, mix coconut starch with 15ml cold water, add to the cooked sauce mixture to make it little thick and serve immediately.

Nutritional Information

- Preparation Time: 30 minutes
- Total Servings: 2
- Calories: 437
- Calories from Fat: 142
- Fat: 15.8g
- Saturated Fat: 7g
- Cholesterol: 101mg
- Carbohydrates: 38.2g
- Fiber: 0.6g
- Sugar: 42.2g
- Protein: 30.3g

Tips to extra flavor

- Before serving, add honey and soy sauce for better taste

Recipe 49: Korean Chicken Thighs

Ingredients

BBQ Sauce:
- Red chili paste 25g
- Hoisin sauce 30ml
- Ketchup 30g
- Mirin 30g
- Fish sauce 30ml
- Vinegar 25ml
- Fresh ginger 7g
- Fresh garlic 3g

Chicken:
- Vegetable oil 14g
- Chicken thighs 450g
- Chopped onion 40g
- Ginger 3g
- Garlic 3g
- Chicken broth 120ml
- Coconut starch 5g
- Water 30ml

Preparation Method

BBQ Sauce:
1. In a medium bowl, add BBQ sauce ingredients and set aside.

Preparing Chicken:

2. Sauté the instant pot cooker and brown the chicken pieces on both sides in the vegetable oil until it turns to golden color. Set aside.
3. Now, add the ginger, garlic, onion and cook until the onion becomes soft. Add the chicken pieces and mixture to the pressure cooker.
4. Mix the chicken broth with the BBQ sauce and add this mixture to cooker. Select cooking timer for 15 minutes on high pressure.
5. Mix the coconut starch with broth and add to the mixture to make the gravy thick.
6. Before serving, remove chicken pieces to a platter. Pour the sauce over the top, and garnish with slice scallions. Serve with jasmine rice.

Nutritional Information

- Preparation Time: 35 minutes
- Total Servings: 2
- Calories: 476
- Calories from Fat: 214
- Fat: 23.8g
- Saturated Fat: 4.8g
- Cholesterol: 71mg
- Sodium: 1150mg
- Potassium: 227mg
- Carbohydrates: 39g
- Fiber: 1.6g
- Sugar: 2.3g
- Protein: 18.5g

Tips to extra flavor

- You can substitute sriracha sauce instead of ketchup

Recipe 50: Pork Loin with Onion Sauce

Ingredients

- Pork loin chops 2 (boneless and 1.25 inches thick slices)
- Small sliced onion 40g
- Olive oil 10g
- Balsamic vinegar 10g
- Worcestershire sauce 10g
- Fish sauce 10g
- Honey 8g
- Chicken stock 100ml
- Coconut starch 10g (mixed in 20ml water)
- Kosher salt to taste

Marinade:

- Light soy sauce 7g
- Shaoxing wine 7g
- Salt 2g
- Honey 2g
- Ground white pepper 2g
- Almond oil 2g

Preparation Method

1. At first, cut pork loin to tenderize the meat and marinate the tenderized pork loin chops for at least 20 minutes with sugar, salt, sesame oil, ground white pepper, fish sauce and Shaoxing wine.

2. Select sauté in your instant pot cooker and when the pot is hot, add olive oil into the pot. Now, add the marinated pork loin chops into the cooker pot and let it brown for 1 minute on each side. Later, remove from cooker and set aside.
3. Now, add sliced onions, salt, and ground black pepper seasonings. Cook the onions for 1 minute or until soften.
4. Add balsamic vinegar, chicken stock, Worcestershire sauce, soy sauce, sugar and mix well until it combined well. Taste the seasoning and if necessary, add missing items.
5. Put your pork loin chops with all the meat juice into the pot. Set your cooker to high pressure for 1 minute.
6. Remove the pork loin chops and keep aside. Press sauté button and taste the seasoning, add more salt if necessary. Mix the coconut starch in little water and add to the onion sauce.
7. Drizzle the onion sauce over the pork loin chops and serve immediately.

Nutritional Information

- Preparation Time: 30 minutes
- Total Servings: 2
- Calories: 345
- Calories from Fat: 69
- Fat: 7.7g
- Saturated Fat: 2.4g
- Cholesterol: 69mg
- Carbohydrates: 39g
- Fiber: 3.7g
- Sugar: 7.9g
- Protein: 22.1g

Tips to extra flavor

- If desired, you can add 14g of honey with onion sauce

Conclusion

The information provided in this book will help you to educate in the right way toward your successful ambition to follow and prepare instant pot recipes to maintain good health throughout your life. Before you start each day, remember and remind yourself about incredible benefits you achieve while the cooking in instant pot and tell yourself that you can do this for improving your health and to avoid future diseases. Once again thank you for downloading our book, and we hope you will achieve your dreams.

Nancy Brown